NATIONAL
GEOGRAPHIC

A Tree for All
Seasons

BY ROBIN BERNARD

SCHOLASTIC INC.
New York   Toronto   London   Auckland   Sydney
Mexico City   New Delhi   Hong Kong   Buenos Aires

For Andy & Liam

☐ NATIONAL
GEOGRAPHIC

ISBN-13: 978-0-545-11385-4
ISBN-10: 0-545-11385-7

12 11 10 9 8 7 6 5 4 3 2 1   8 9 10 11 12 13/0

Printed in the U.S.A.   08

First Scholastic printing, September 2008

Produced through the worldwide resources of the National Geographic Society,
John M. Fahey, Jr., *President and CEO*; Gilbert M. Grosvenor, *Chairman of the
Board*; Nina D. Hoffman, *Senior Vice President, Publications*.

Prepared by the Education Division, Ericka Markman, *Vice President and Director*.

Staff for this book: Lori Dibble Collins, *Editor*; Carolyn Hatt, *Release Editor*;
Robin Bernard, *Writer*; James Hiscott, Jr., *Art Director*;
Paula Dailey, *Picture Editor*; Molly Leach, *Designer*; Jean Cantu, *Coordinator*.

Consultants: Dr. Frank S. Santamour, Jr., *U.S. National Arboretum*;
Donna Driscoll, *Teacher, Montgomery County Public Schools, MD*;
Debbie Korth, *Reading Specialist, Montgomery County Public Schools, MD*;
Kristen Samonsky, *Teacher, Montgomery County Public Schools, MD*;
Thana Vance, *Language Arts Specialist, Reading K-12, Arlington Public Schools, VA*.

Year after year, a maple tree changes from season to season.

In winter the tree is bare. It looks dead, but it is alive and well. Many things are happening.

A little bird sits
on a branch and
calls its name:
Chicka-dee-dee-dee!

Squirrels nap in a
cozy tree hole.

Look closely at this tree
branch. The bumps at the
tip are buds. They will
open into leaves when the
weather gets warmer.

As winter ends, nights are still cold, but days are getting warmer.

It is perfect weather for farmers to collect sugar maple sap.

The sap flows out of taps and into buckets.

The sap has no color until it is boiled. Then it becomes dark sweet maple syrup.

What a treat for pancakes and waffles!

Spring brings warmer weather.

The leaf buds open.

Soon the maple
tree grows
floppy green
flower tassels.

Birds build
nests on the
branches.

Spring also brings rain showers.

The tree's roots soak up water and carry it to all parts of the tree.

Sunshine
helps the tree
make sap, which
feeds the tree.

Look at the
veins in a leaf.
Air, water,
and sap all
flow
through
them.

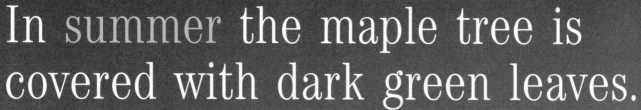

In summer the maple tree is covered with dark green leaves.

Fruit, called samaras, is growing on the tree. It makes a good meal for a chipmunk.

Even on a hot summer day, you can find a cool place to play under a maple tree.

In autumn the tree's leaves turn bright colors.

As the leaves dry up, they change from green to yellow, red, and orange. Each day more and more leaves fall.

Autumn brings chilly days and nights.

Bugs crawl under the tree's bark where they will sleep through the cold weather.

Animals
get ready
for winter
when food
will be hard to find.
Squirrels hide lots
of nuts and seeds.

If you play in the leaves you'll hear
crunch, scrunch, crunch! But don't
worry about making noise. The maple tree
won't wake up again until spring.

![National Geographic logo] **NATIONAL GEOGRAPHIC**